ISBN: 978-0-9966685-8-3
WWW.HERMANITYPROJECT.COM

PUBLISHED & DESIGNED BY: HOLON PUBLISHING

A PUBLISHING COMPANY AND CREATIVE COLLECTIVE AIMED AT EMPOWERING AUTHORS, ARTISTS, BUSINESSES, NON-PROFITS, AND THEIR SURROUNDING COMMUNITIES.

FOR MORE INFORMATION ABOUT JOINING THIS COMMUNITY, OR ORDERING ADDITIONAL COPIES OF THE HERMANITY PROJECT, VISIT THE PUBLISHER'S WEBSITE:

WWW.HOLON.CO

OR FOLLOW HOLON ON TWITTER:
@HOLONPUBLISHING

THE HERMANITY PROJECT

STRATEGIES
FOR A LIVING PLANET

YOU ARE EVERYONE
AND EVERYONE IS YOU

Michael Gione

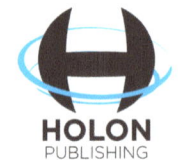

HOLON
PUBLISHING

"Each being contains in itself the whole intelligible world. Therefore All is everywhere. Each is there All, and All is each. Man as he now is has ceased to be the All. But when he ceases to be an individual, he raises himself again and penetrates the whole world."

- Plotinus

CONTENTS

EXISTENCE IS
FREEDOM

FREEDOM IS
CREATIVITY

CREATIVITY IS
EXCELLENCE

SOMEWHERE BETWEEN THE
BREATH OF OUR FIRST DAYS
AND THE
SUN OF OUR LAST
WE WALK AMONG OUR OWN

WE WORK WE PLAY
WE LOVE WE DIE

PERHAPS THROUGH IT ALL THERE IS
A WAY THAT WE CAN LEAVE THIS
LIFE A LITTLE BETTER FOR HAVING
BEEN HERE

JUDGMENT

I LIVE IN JUDGMENT OF NO ONE

JUDGMENT IS THE GROWTH OF EGO

I JUDGE TO BUILD MYSELF

JUDGMENT IS EASY, ALL THAT IS NECESSARY
IS THE SHUTTING OF ONE'S MIND AND THE DEAFNESS
OF ONE'S EAR

JUDGING YOURSELF FIRST WILL CREATE
AN UNDERSTANDING FOR YOUR NEIGHBOR

WHEN I JUDGE MY NEIGHBOR I AM
ALSO JUDGING MYSELF

JUDGE YOURSELF AS YOU JUDGE OTHERS

I JUDGE NOT MY NEIGHBOR'S FAULTS

JUDGMENT IS THE SKILL OF IGNORANCE

WHEN I STING MY NEIGHBOR FOR HIS INSULTS
I THEN BECOME MY NEIGHBOR

WHEN YOU JUDGE THE BULLY, ARE YOU
REALLY REMEMBERING YOURSELF ?

JUSTICE

I FIGHT IN JUSTICE FOR ALL

RIGHTEOUS MEN ARE LONG IN THOUGHT
AND QUICK TO ACTION

WHEN I AM RIGHTEOUS FOR MYSELF I THEN CHOOSE
JUSTICE FOR ALL OTHERS

DO YOU LEND YOUR HAND IN RIGHTEOUSNESS ?

LET GO YOUR EGO TO EXTEND JUSTICE TO ALL

JUSTICE MUST PREVAIL AT ALL COST

DO I SEE MY NEIGHBOR AS MYSELF ?

EQUALITY IS THE TRUE SEED OF JUSTICE

DO YOU LEND YOUR HAND IN RIGHTEOUSNESS ?

I JUDGE NOT MY NEIGHBOR'S FAULTS

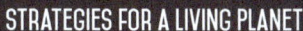

JUSTICE IS THE OPEN DOOR
OF UNDERSTANDING

WHEN WE ARE RIGHTEOUS
WE OFTEN STAND ALONE

JUDGEMENT IS THE SKILL OF IGNORANCE

DO I STAND COURAGEOUS ?

LOVE

I AM RELENTLESS IN MY SEARCH FOR LOVE

THE SEED OF LOVE MUST GROW
BEFORE IT WILL APPEAR

WHEN YOU LOVE OTHERS YOU LOVE THAT
WHICH YOU HAVE BECOME

DOES YOUR LOVE ESCAPE YOU
OR HOLD YOU FAST ?

LOVE IS THE CAVERN DEEP,
WIDE, AND RIPE WITH HOPE

LOVE LIVES WITH THOSE WHO
WILL FEEL ITS WARMTH

WHEN YOU LOVE YOU ARE SHUTTING OUT THE DARK

THE KIND OF PERSON WE NEED TO BE
IS TO LOVE AND BE LOVED AS WELL

YOUR LOVE WILL COLOR YOU MORE,
THE COLOR YOU ARE

I KNOW MYSELF AND THEN I AM LOVED

WHAT IS IT THAT REMINDS YOU OF YOURSELF
IS IT FEAR, ANGER, OR IS IT LOVE ?

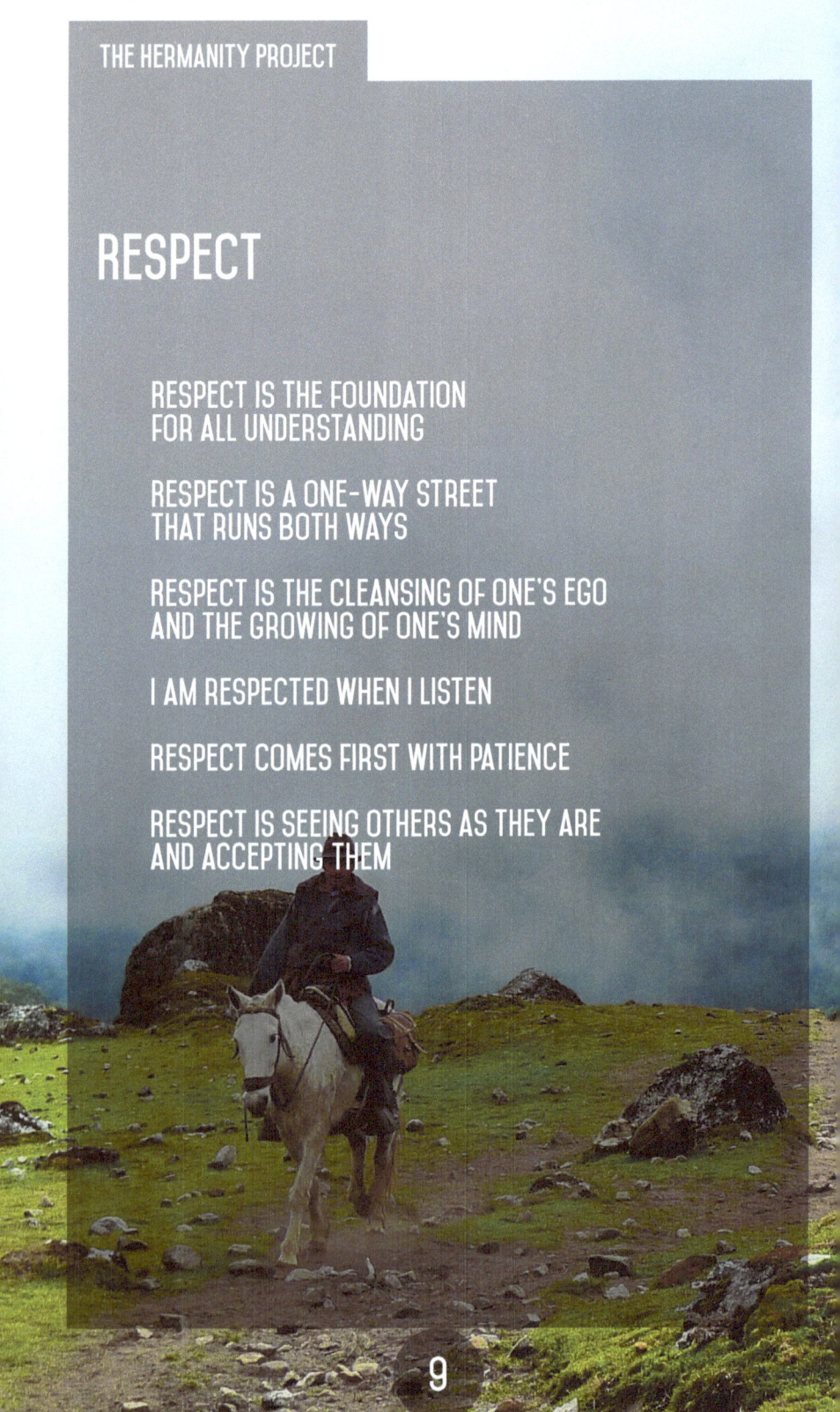

RESPECT

RESPECT IS THE FOUNDATION
FOR ALL UNDERSTANDING

RESPECT IS A ONE-WAY STREET
THAT RUNS BOTH WAYS

RESPECT IS THE CLEANSING OF ONE'S EGO
AND THE GROWING OF ONE'S MIND

I AM RESPECTED WHEN I LISTEN

RESPECT COMES FIRST WITH PATIENCE

RESPECT IS SEEING OTHERS AS THEY ARE
AND ACCEPTING THEM

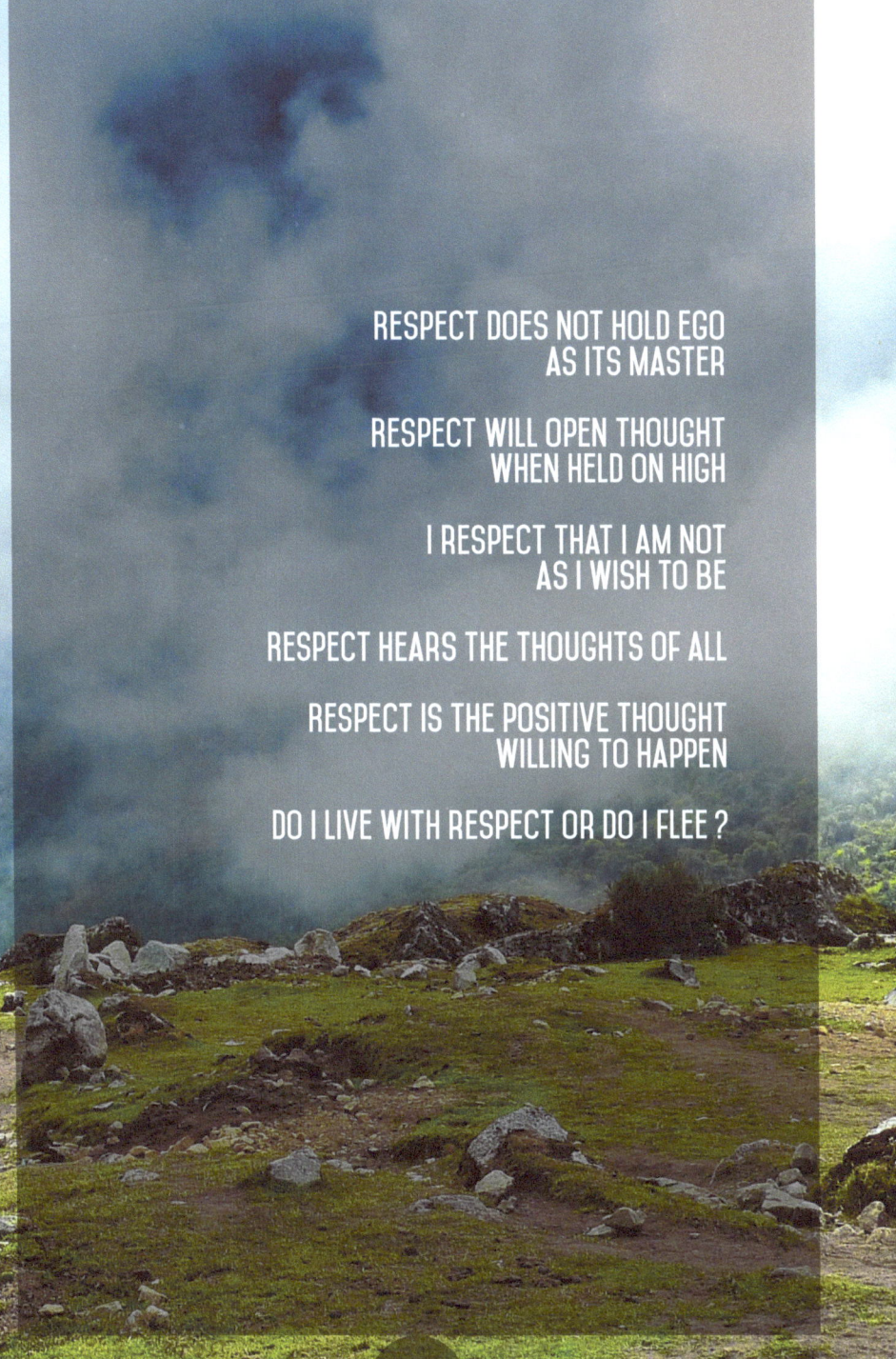

RESPECT DOES NOT HOLD EGO
AS ITS MASTER

RESPECT WILL OPEN THOUGHT
WHEN HELD ON HIGH

I RESPECT THAT I AM NOT
AS I WISH TO BE

RESPECT HEARS THE THOUGHTS OF ALL

RESPECT IS THE POSITIVE THOUGHT
WILLING TO HAPPEN

DO I LIVE WITH RESPECT OR DO I FLEE ?

COMPROMISE

I EMBRACE COMPROMISE AS A TOOL FOR CHANGE

COLORS THAT COME TOGETHER AND
SEEK THE HAND OUTSTRETCHED

COMPROMISE IS LEAVING ONE'S ARGUMENT
FOR THE GOOD OF THE CAUSE

COMPROMISE IS THE DARK OF NIGHT
YIELDING TO THE LIGHT OF DAY

COMPROMISE IS THE SKILL OF TURNING EVEN WHEN
ALL HOPE IS LOST

COMPROMISE IS THE FIGHTING SPIRIT
THAT BENDS TO WIN

TO COMPROMISE WE MUST FIRST
LISTEN TO ALL NEEDS

COMPROMISE DOES NOT MEAN WEAKNESS

COMPROMISE IS THE FOOD OF GROWTH

CAN I TRULY COMPROMISE WHEN
I AM UNWILLING TO LISTEN ?

PREJUDICE

I REFUSE ALL PREJUDICE FOR MYSELF
AND ALL OTHERS

ON THE PATH OF PREJUDICE ONE MUST IGNORE ALL FACT

PREJUDICE WILL HALT THE GROWTH OF ONE'S MIND

IGNORANCE IS THE FUEL OF PREJUDICE

I AM BLIND WHEN I REFUSE TO HEAR MY NEIGHBOR

PREJUDICE CANNOT EXIST
WITHOUT CARE AND NOURISHMENT

I EXCLUDE FROM MY LIFE ALL THOUGHTS
THAT WILL PREJUDICE MYSELF AND OTHERS

I GROW PREJUDICE WHEN I WORSHIP MYSELF

PREJUDICE CANNOT EXIST IN
THE LIGHT OF UNDERSTANDING

PREJUDICE IS THE WALL THAT LOCKS
OUT ONE'S THOUGHTS

PREJUDICE TAKES TIME, ENERGY,
AND MISGUIDED THOUGHT

PREJUDICE IS NOT SIMPLY SOMETHING WE DO,
PREJUDICE IS SOMETHING WE PRACTICE TO DO WELL

I FAIL WHEN I BELIEVE THAT I HAVE REACHED
MY FULL POTENTIAL, YET I AM STILL PREJUDICED

I ADMIT MY PREJUDICE YET I STAND FOR TRUTH

ARE WE ALL PREJUDICED ?

DETERMINATION

I AM DETERMINED FOR THE FREEDOM OF ALL

DETERMINATION IS THE SIMPLE ACT OF
BELIEVING IN VICTORY

DETERMINATION IS AS THE GROWING TREE,
EVER REACHING TOWARD THE SKY

DETERMINATION IS THE MIND OF DAVID
IN THE BODY OF GOLIATH

THE WILLPOWER OF THE MOUNTAIN AND
THE TRANQUILITY OF THE DEEP

THE RESOLVE OF THE FALCON LOCKED IN FLIGHT

A COURSE OF ACTION CHOSEN
WELL AND FOLLOWED THROUGH

DETERMINATION IS THE ACT OF STAYING
THE PATH EVEN AGAINST ALL ODDS

DETERMINATION IS THE STRENGTH OF MIND
AND THE POWER OF AMBITION

DETERMINATION IS FIRST THE LETTING GO OF PAIN

DO I LIVE DETERMINED ?

TRUST

I BRING TRUST TO ALL

I GO BLIND INTO THE NIGHT AND SO I TRUST
THAT OTHERS WILL FIND ME

TO FIND MYSELF I WILL REACH OUT MY HAND,
EVEN IN THE DARK

I ACCEPT THE WORDS OF APOLOGY
AND REFUSE THE CRITICAL FACE

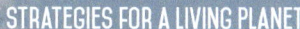

I BUILD TRUST WHEN I BELIEVE IN FREEDOM FOR ALL

THERE IS NO TRUST WITHOUT UNDERSTANDING

DO I BRING TRUST TO MY LIFE ?

FEAR

I STAND AS A WARRIOR AGAINST ALL FEAR

WHEN WE FEAR WE ASSUME THAT WE HAVE
THE RIGHT TO BE AFRAID

FEAR IS THE BELIEF THAT I AM NOT AS I NEED TO BE

FEAR IS THE BELIEF THAT WE ARE ALONE
WE ARE NOT

WHAT YOU FEAR IS FILLING UP YOUR LIFE
AND DIMINISHING YOUR
ACCEPTANCE AND ABILITY TO LOVE

WHEN YOU ARE REFUSING LOVE
YOU WEAR YOUR FEAR AS A BADGE

WHEN WE FEAR WE JUDGE OURSELVES AND OTHERS

THE ABSENCE OF FEAR IS IN THE
LOOSENING OF CONTROL

FEAR IS THE ABSENCE OF HOPE

WHAT IS IT THAT REMINDS YOU OF YOURSELF
IS IT FEAR, ANGER, OR IS IT ACCEPTANCE ?

CONTENTMENT

I AM CONTENT IN LEARNING FROM OTHERS

I AM CONTENT THAT EVERYONE MUST PROSPER

I AM CONTENT IN THAT I AM WILLING TO LEARN

I AM CONTENT THAT ALL
PEOPLE DESERVE UNDERSTANDING

I AM NEVER CONTENT IN MY IGNORANCE

I AM CONTENT THAT I CAN ALWAYS LEARN

I AM CONTENT IN MY BELIEF THAT
MY NEIGHBOR IS MYSELF

I AM CONTENT IN SHARING HOPE WITH ALL

AM I CONTENT WITH MY PLACE OF
RESPONSIBILITY IN THIS WORLD ?

FREEDOM

EXISTENCE IS FREEDOM

EXISTENCE IS FREEDOM FOR ALL

I WILL GUARANTEE MY NEIGHBOR'S FREEDOM

FREEDOM IS NEVER A PRIVILEGE

EXISTENCE GUARANTEES FREEDOM

I SHARE THE HOPE OF FREEDOM FOR ALL

OUR BIRTH GUARANTEES OUR FREEDOM

TO EVERYONE THERE IS FREEDOM,
EVEN AGAINST ALL REFUSAL

FREEDOM IS A BELIEF SYSTEM
THAT ONLY I CAN REFUSE

TRUE BELIEF IN FREEDOM IGNITES CREATIVITY

WE MUST FIRST BELIEVE IN FREEDOM FOR OURSELVES,
THEN WE WILL SEE FREEDOM FOR ALL OTHERS

LIVE FREE TO EMBRACE YOURSELF

IT IS NOT A PRIVILEGE TO DENY MY NEIGHBOR'S
FREEDOM — IT IS A DECISION

DO YOU TRULY BELIEVE IN FREEDOM
FOR ALL OTHERS ?

POSSIBILITIES

I SEE IN MY NEIGHBOR ALL THAT IS POSSIBLE

FOR ALL TO PROSPER ALL MUST FIRST BELIEVE

IS IT POSSIBLE TO LEARN WITHOUT FIRST
UNDERSTANDING YOUR NEIGHBOR ?

ALL THINGS ARE POSSIBLE IN PARTNERSHIP

FIRST YOU MUST LET GO OF PREJUDICE AND
THEN YOU WILL SEE POSSIBILITIES FOR FREEDOM

IS IT POSSIBLE THAT I PROSPER
YET LEARN NOTHING ?

CREATIVITY

FREEDOM ALLOWS CREATIVITY

CREATIVITY IS GROUNDED IN FREEDOM
AND IN EXCELLENCE

CREATIVITY IS IN THE HEART OF ALL WHO LIVE

CREATIVITY IS THE ROAD TO
GROWTH AND EXCELLENCE

FREEDOM WILL CREATE EXCELLENCE

I AM CREATIVE WHEN I FIND CREATIVITY IN ALL

CREATIVITY IS THOUGHT IN ACTION

I LEAD THE WAY WHEN I EXPRESS CREATIVITY

AM I CREATIVE ENOUGH FOR MY NEIGHBOR'S LIFE ?

DO I SUPPORT MY NEIGHBOR'S CREATIVITY ?

GUARANTEE

FOR ALL MEN I GUARANTEE FREEDOM

MY FREEDOM IS GUARANTEED WHEN I
OBSERVE FREEDOM FOR ALL OTHERS

MY PROMISE IS TO GUARANTEE CREATIVITY
IN MYSELF AND OTHERS

I AM GUARANTEED CREATIVITY BY THE FREEDOM
I PRACTICE FOR ALL

FREEDOM, CREATIVITY, AND EXCELLENCE ARE
THE PROMISE FOR ALL

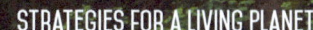

I GUARANTEE FIRST MY NEEDS AND THEN
I GUARANTEE ALL OTHERS

I GUARANTEE NOTHING WITHOUT ACTION

AS I MOVE THROUGH THE REALITY OF MY
NEIGHBOR'S LIFE, WHAT WILL I GUARANTEE ?

EXCELLENCE

IN CREATIVITY THERE IS EXCELLENCE

I WILL BE EXCELLENT IN MY
APPROACH TOWARD ALL OTHERS

EXCELLENCE COMES TO LIFE IN ONE'S ACTIONS

EXCELLENCE IS THE ACT OF TREATING
ALL OTHERS AS ONESELF

I AM ONLY EXCELLENT WHEN I SEE
EXCELLENCE IN OTHERS

EXCELLENCE IS THE GIFT OF
YOUR SPIRIT GIVEN FREELY

WILL I PRACTICE EXCELLENCE ?

BELIEF

BELIEF IN MYSELF ALLOWS FOR BELIEF IN OTHERS

BELIEF IS THE ABILITY TO SEE MY LIFE TOMORROW

WHEN MY NEIGHBOR WALKS IN MY SHADOW
DOES HE BELIEVE THAT I WILL PROTECT HIM ?

BELIEF DOES NOT RESIDE ONLY IN THE MIND
BELIEF RESIDES IN THE HEART AS WELL

CAN YOUR BELIEF SET YOU FREE ?

DO I TAKE ACTION WITH MY BELIEFS ?

GROWTH

I GROW MYSELF AS I GROW MY NEIGHBOR

GROWTH WILL COME WITH UNDERSTANDING,
UNDERSTANDING WILL COME WITH COMPASSION,
COMPASSION IS THE SEED

MY POTENTIAL FOR GROWTH IS FIRST MY
POTENTIAL TO GROW MY NEIGHBOR

THERE IS GROWTH IN LISTENING TO OTHERS

GROWTH BECOMES POSSIBLE WITH AN OPEN MIND

WILL I TAKE ACTION TO GROW ?

RESPONSIBILITY

I AM RESPONSIBLE FOR MY ACTIONS

I AM RESPONSIBLE WHEN I REMEMBER
THE VOICE OF MY NEIGHBOR

RESPONSIBILITY COMES FIRST
WITH POSITIVE THOUGHT

IS RESPONSIBILITY YOUR OBLIGATION
AND YOUR CAUSE ?

IN DOING GOOD WORKS YOU WILL
STRENGTHEN YOUR LIFE

LIFE KNOWS NO BOUNDARIES WHEN WE
ACT RESPONSIBLY WITH OTHERS

DO I TAKE CHARGE OF MY DESTINY ?

SING LOUD TO LIFE'S RESPONSIBILITY

WHERE DO I FEAR TO GO
WITH MY RESPONSIBILITY ?

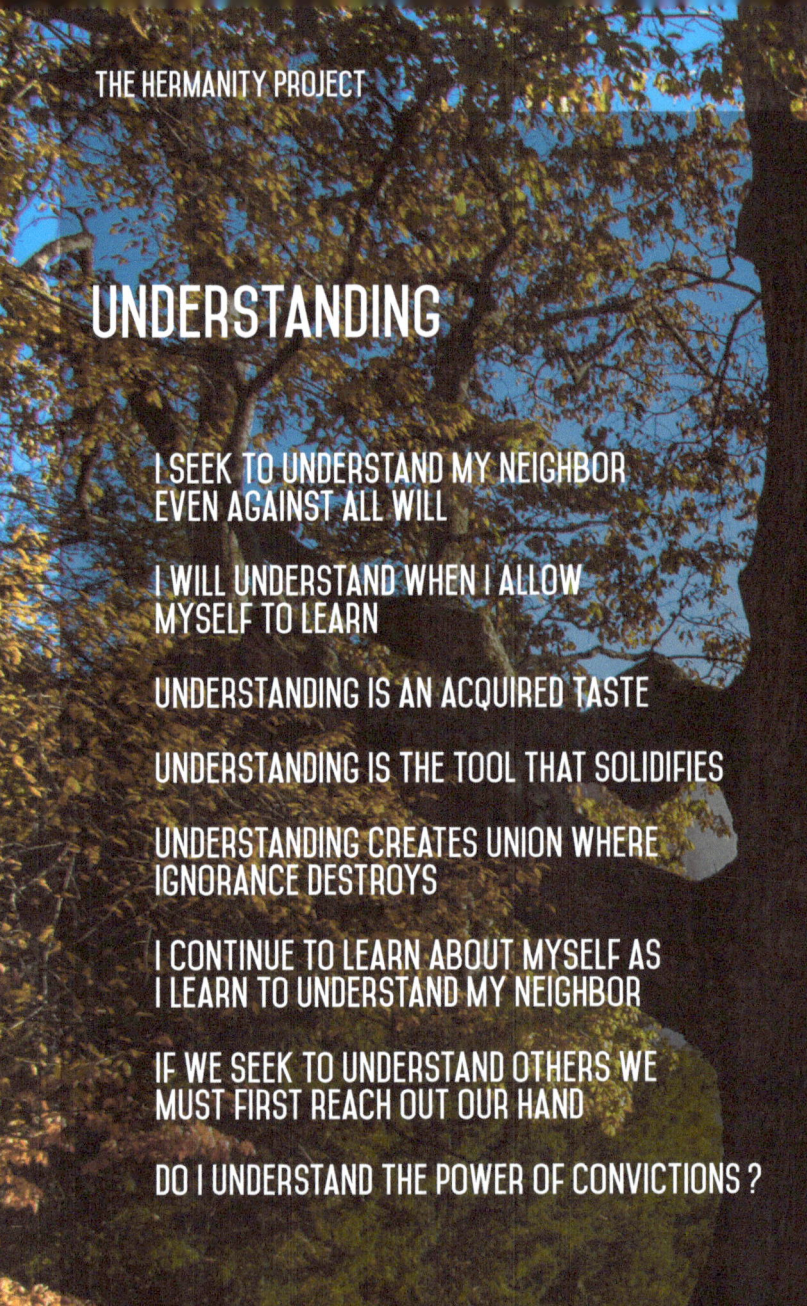

UNDERSTANDING

I SEEK TO UNDERSTAND MY NEIGHBOR
EVEN AGAINST ALL WILL

I WILL UNDERSTAND WHEN I ALLOW
MYSELF TO LEARN

UNDERSTANDING IS AN ACQUIRED TASTE

UNDERSTANDING IS THE TOOL THAT SOLIDIFIES

UNDERSTANDING CREATES UNION WHERE
IGNORANCE DESTROYS

I CONTINUE TO LEARN ABOUT MYSELF AS
I LEARN TO UNDERSTAND MY NEIGHBOR

IF WE SEEK TO UNDERSTAND OTHERS WE
MUST FIRST REACH OUT OUR HAND

DO I UNDERSTAND THE POWER OF CONVICTIONS ?

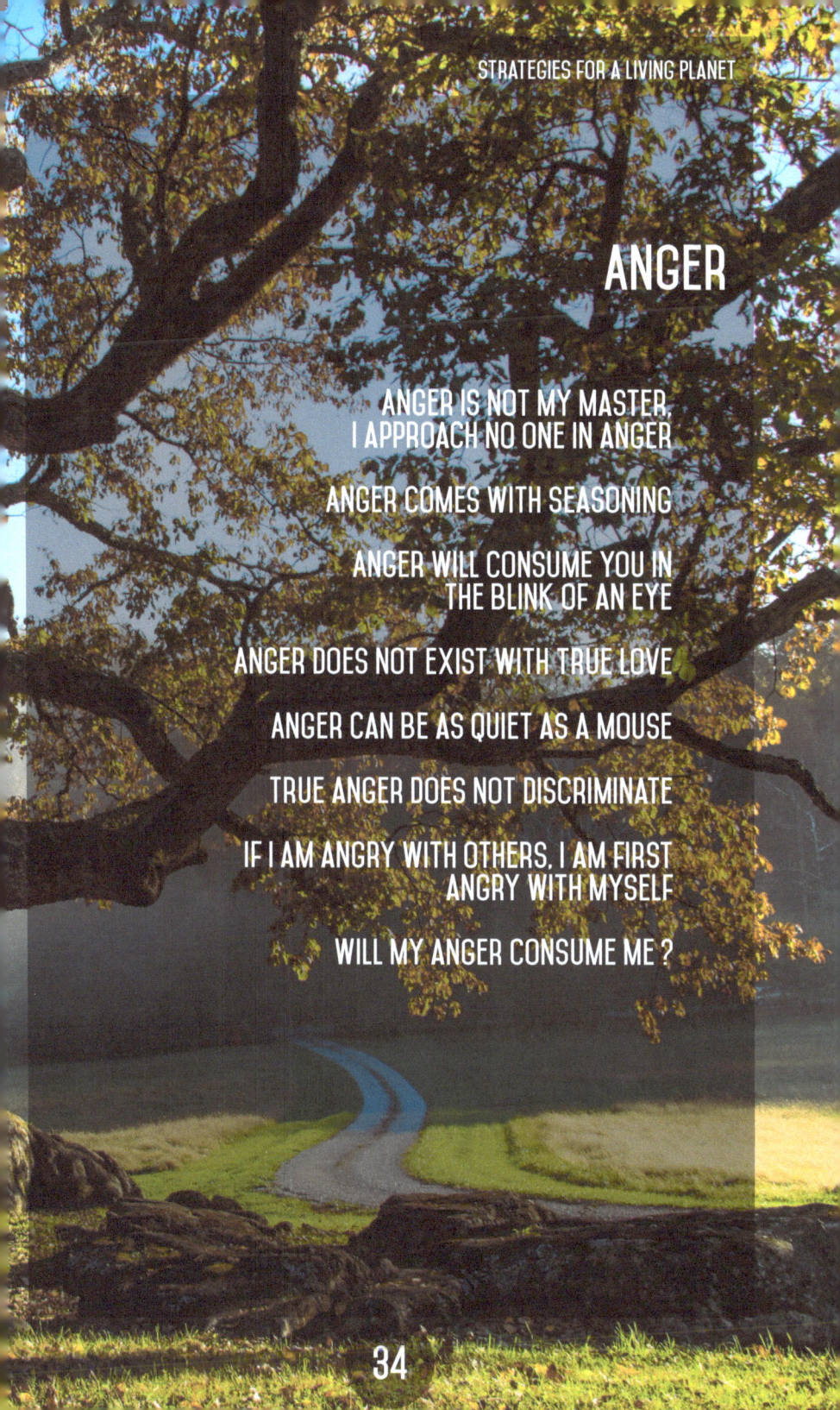

ANGER

ANGER IS NOT MY MASTER,
I APPROACH NO ONE IN ANGER

ANGER COMES WITH SEASONING

ANGER WILL CONSUME YOU IN
THE BLINK OF AN EYE

ANGER DOES NOT EXIST WITH TRUE LOVE

ANGER CAN BE AS QUIET AS A MOUSE

TRUE ANGER DOES NOT DISCRIMINATE

IF I AM ANGRY WITH OTHERS, I AM FIRST
ANGRY WITH MYSELF

WILL MY ANGER CONSUME ME ?

HATE

I TEACH NOT NOR APPROACH NOT IN HATE

HATE IS THE ENGINE OF BIGOTRY

HATE WILL REACH ALL WHO RELISH IGNORANCE

I HATE OTHERS WHEN I FEAR CHANGE

HATE WILL SEIZE YOUR THOUGHTS AND
SLING YOU DOWN

NOTHING IS WORTHWHILE WITH HATE
AS ITS MASTER

NO ONE HATES WITHOUT CHOICE

I DECIDE TO HATE MY NEIGHBOR

DO I APPROACH WITH HARM ?

FAITH

I CONTINUE IN FAITH FOR MY NEIGHBOR

DO I REALLY BELIEVE A STRANGER
WILL COMFORT ME ?

DO I REALLY BELIEVE I WILL
COMFORT A STRANGER ?

FAITH IS BLIND TO CRITICISM

FAITH IS BELIEF WITHOUT FACT

WE BELIEVE IN OUR OWN FAITH,
DO WE BELIEVE IN OTHERS ?

TO HAVE FAITH I MUST TAKE ACTION

IN FAITH FOR MY NEIGHBOR I LEND A BLIND HAND

DOES MY FAITH ALLOW AND
STRENGTHEN MY NEIGHBOR ?

DISCOVERY

WE MUST FIRST DISCOVER OURSELVES BEFORE WE
ARE DISCOVERED

TO DISCOVER YOUR NEIGHBOR YOU MUST
OPEN YOUR MIND

DISCOVERY IS IGNITED BY FREEDOM

DISCOVERY IS LIMITED BY YOUR COMPASSION

IF YOU REFUSE TO DISCOVER THE STRANGER
YOU WILL LOSE YOUR WAY

EACH DAY I CHOOSE TO DISCOVER MY FAITH

ARE YOU WILLING TO DISCOVER YOUR WEAKNESS ?

ARE YOU WILLING TO DISCOVER EACH DAY ?

HEART

WITH HEART I FULFILL MY LOVE

CAN YOUR HEART DEFEAT YOU ?

WE SPEAK WITH OUR MIND, WE
TOUCH WITH OUR HEART

DO WE LEND OUR HEARTS TO OUR
NEIGHBOR'S CAUSE ?

TO HAVE HEART IS TO FIGHT ON

THE HEART OF HOPE WILL DEFEAT
THE MIND OF DOUBT.

THOSE WHO ARE HEARTLESS WILL REMAIN
LOST IN DARKNESS

DO I OPENLY SHARE MY COMPASSION ?

WHAT OF MY LIFE LEADS BACK
TO THE HEART ?

INTEGRITY

DISHONESTY IS THE OPPOSITE OF INTEGRITY

IT IS WITH INTEGRITY THAT I LIVE MY LIFE

INTEGRITY IS BEING TRUE TO ONESELF

IN TRUTH I MEET MY NEIGHBORS ON THE
ROAD OF LIFE

INTEGRITY LIVES IN ALL OF US

WE NEED NOT FIGHT AGAINST HONOR,
HONOR WILL EVENTUALLY WIN

IS MY INTEGRITY FACING MY NEIGHBOR ?

DO I BELIEVE IN MY NEIGHBOR'S INTEGRITY ?

INTEGRITY KNOWS NO COMPROMISE

DO I BRING HONOR TO MY LIFE ?

ACCEPTANCE

I WILL ACCEPT MYSELF FIRST

WITHOUT ACCEPTANCE THERE IS NO LOVE

IN BLINDNESS I AGREE TO ACCEPT
MY NEIGHBOR'S DIFFERENCES

I BRING ACCEPTANCE TO ALL THAT I DO

I ACCEPT ALL ARGUMENTS AS MY OWN

WHAT I ACCEPT WITH MY WORDS I MUST
ACT WITH MY HEART

ACCEPTANCE IS EASY FROM ONE'S MOUTH,
BUT DIFFICULT IN ONE'S DEEDS

I REACH OUT EVEN TO MY ENEMY FOR
I AM HIS ENEMY AS WELL

ACCEPTANCE IS LETTING GO OF ONE'S EGO

DO I TRULY ACCEPT MYSELF ?

PEACE

IN PEACE WE FACE EACH OTHER

DO I SEE STILLNESS IN MY NEIGHBOR'S LIFE ?

PEACE WILL CURE ILLS THAT CURSE US ALL

IN MY LONGING FOR PEACE ALL MUST BE INCLUDED

I SEEK PEACE WITH DETERMINATION AND HOPE

WHY DO WE SEEK OUR OWN EGOS AND
NOT THE PEACE OF LIGHT ?

WHEN WE COME TOGETHER IN PEACE
WE SATISFY OUR HEART'S DESIRE

PEACE IS NOT AN EASY TURN BUT
ONE WE TURN TO WIN

WHICH PART OF PEACE WILL EMBARRASS ?

OUR DESIRE FOR PEACE MUST REACH ALL WHO EXIST

FOR WHOM DO YOU NOT WISH PEACE AND WHY ?

EGO

MY HURTFUL EGO SHALL NOT BRUISE MY NEIGHBOR

AN EGO CAN BE AS A GIANT,
FILLED TO THE BRIM

WHAT CAN I DO WITH A HEALING EGO ?

HOW DO WE MOVE OUR EGO FROM
OURSELVES TO OUR NEIGHBOR ?

DO I NOT KNOW THAT MY SELF-IMAGE
IS AS I WISH IT TO BE ?

EGO CAN RUSH IN WITH DOORS CLOSED SHUT

AN EGO CAN BE A FRESH BREATH OF HOPE

EGOS CAN HEAL OR THEY CAN HARM

WITHIN MY EGO THERE MUST BE ROOM
FOR MY NEIGHBOR

IF I CLING TO MY FAULTLESS EGO
WHERE DO I GROW ?

I WILL GROW AWAY FROM THE GREED OF EGO

DO I BRUISE WITH MY EGO OR DO I HEAL ?

GOSSIP

GOSSIP DESTROYS ALL THAT IT SEES

WHEN I BRING GOSSIP I DESTROY RELATIONSHIPS

GOSSIP IS AS THE DARK OF NIGHT

WHEN WE GOSSIP WE ARE USING OUR
TIME TO TEAR DOWN

I DO NOT SPEAK TRUTH WHEN I
SPEAK OF GOSSIP

WHAT PART OF MY INTEGRITY SPEAKS THE
WORDS OF GOSSIP ?

WHEN I GOSSIP I LIE WITH MY SPEECH

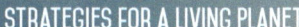

AM I WILLING TO SPEAK FORWARD IN THOUGHT ?

HAVE I LEARNED FROM THE MISTAKE OF GOSSIP ?

WHAT REWARD COMES FROM GOSSIP ?

DO I REALLY BELIEVE THAT GOSSIP DESTROYS ?

LEARNING

LEARNING MUST BE AS THE BREATH OF LIFE

LEARNING IS THE OPENING OF ONE'S
MIND AND HEART

AM I TRULY WILLING TO LEARN FROM OTHERS ?

TRUE KNOWLEDGE DOES NOT KNOW HOUR OR DAY

HOW DOES LEARNING FROM MY NEIGHBOR
BUILD MY LIFE ?

WILL I LEARN AS I TEACH THE STRANGER
IN MY LIFE ?

VOICE

IN ONE VOICE WE BUILD A POSITIVE FUTURE

IS YOUR HELPFUL VOICE CLEAR
OR MUFFLED IN THE DARK ?

THE VOICE OF THE FAIR HAS MUCH
TO BE HEARD

LONELY IS THE VOICE OF COMPASSION

DO I KNOW WHO I WILL HURT BEFORE I SPEAK ?

A VOICE UNHEARD IS IN NEED OF A MESSAGE

DO I USE MY VOICE TO ATTACK MY NEIGHBOR ?

DO I UNDERSTAND THE POWER OF VOICE ? TWO
VOICES THAT SPEAK AT ONCE LEAVE
MUCH IN THE WIND

THE ARGUING VOICE HAS MUCH TO SAY,
BUT LITTLE TO BE HEARD

WITH MY VOICE, I REMAIN ON THIS JOURNEY

AS WE WALK IN ONE VOICE WE
PROSPER AS ONE

DOES YOUR VOICE LIFT UP YOUR NEIGHBOR ?

DO YOU SPEAK THE VOICE OF YOUR HEART ?

MOTHER EARTH

THE EARTH IS MOTHER TO US ALL

FROM THE EARTH WE RISE TO LIFE

IN AN INSTANT WE LIVE AND DIE, THE
EARTH LIVES FOREVER

WHAT ON THIS EARTH DO WE LEAVE BEHIND ?

FOR ALL TO PROSPER WE MUST LIVE UPON THIS
EARTH AS ONE

ON THIS HOME WE CELEBRATE OUR LIFE

WHEN WE FEED THE EARTH WE CAUSE OUR FUTURE

DO WE FEED THE EARTH AS OUR OWN ?

WOMEN

WOMEN ARE THE BACKBONE OF THE EARTH

WOMEN WILL DO WHAT MEN WILL NOT

WOMEN OFTEN DO NOT SUFFER THE EGO OF MEN

THE EARTH LISTENS TO THE VOICE OF ALL MOTHERS

WHO IS IT THAT CAUSES LOVE IN ITS PUREST FORM ?

MEN DO NOT FAIL AT THE FEET OF WOMEN

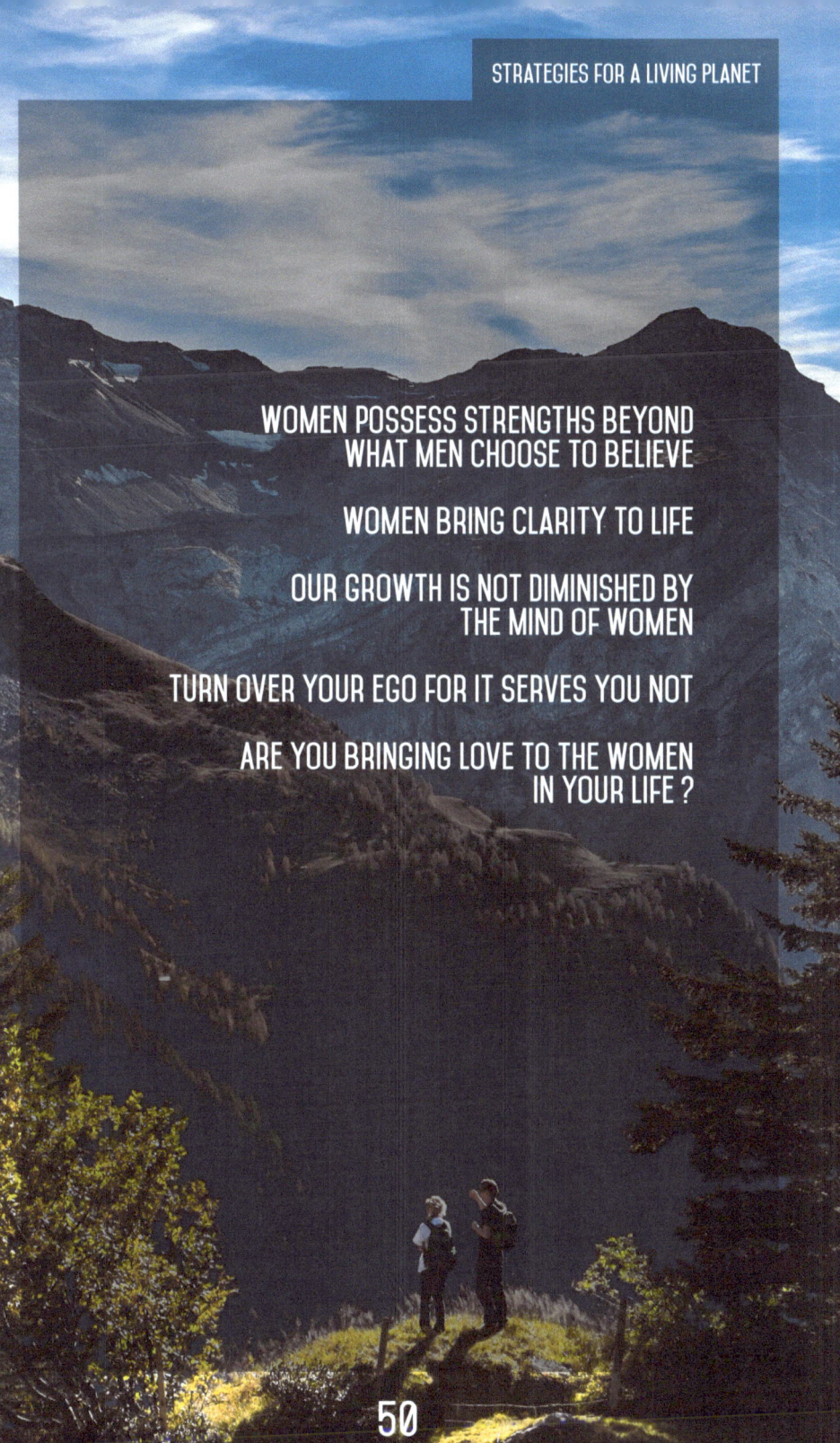

WOMEN POSSESS STRENGTHS BEYOND
WHAT MEN CHOOSE TO BELIEVE

WOMEN BRING CLARITY TO LIFE

OUR GROWTH IS NOT DIMINISHED BY
THE MIND OF WOMEN

TURN OVER YOUR EGO FOR IT SERVES YOU NOT

ARE YOU BRINGING LOVE TO THE WOMEN
IN YOUR LIFE ?

PROSPERITY

THERE IS NO TRUE PROSPERITY WITHOUT COMPASSION

YOUR PROSPERITY SHOULD NEVER CHALLENGE YOUR NEIGHBOR

TO THE FOOL, LOVING PROSPERITY IS UNATTAINABLE

YOUR WISHES AND YOUR DREAMS ARE YOUR NEIGHBOR'S AS WELL

MY RICHES ARE FLEETING, MY LOVE IS NOT

PROSPERITY IS A LEARNING TOOL

PROSPERITY IS NEVER OF RICHES ALONE

YOUR THOUGHTS OF PEACE ARE YOUR TRUE PROSPERITY

AM I TRULY CAPABLE OF SHARING MY PROSPERITY ?

FORGIVENESS

LOVE IS THE ROAD TO FORGIVENESS

THE FORGIVENESS WE HOLD FOR OURSELVES
IS THE COMPASSION WE HAVE FOR ALL OTHERS

IN ANGER WE DRAW MANY COWARDS

IN THE EXCELLENCE OF FORGIVENESS,
WE MAY STAND ALONE

IT IS NOT IN OUR NATURE TO FORGIVE,
IT IS IN OUR NATURE TO JUDGE

WE TALK OF FORGIVENESS YET
SHRINK TO THE TASK

WHERE DO WE FIRST FIND FORGIVENESS

FORGIVENESS IS THE DESTINATION OF THE HEART

CARE NOT THAT YOUR NEIGHBOR DOES
NOT LIVE WITH COMPASSION,
YOUR OWN IS ENOUGH FOR BOTH

DOES YOUR COMPASSION EMBARRASS YOU ?

52

IDOLATRY

IN WHOSE NAME DO YOU IDOLIZE ?

IDOLATRY IS THE FRUIT OF GREED

DO NOT WORSHIP THE POWER OF THAT
WHICH YOU CAN NEVER ACHIEVE

IN SERVICE TO OTHERS,
I PROVE IDOLATRY A FLEETING JOURNEY

TAKE CARE IN YOUR LIFE THAT YOU DO
NOT BECOME A WASTE OF TIME AT
THE WINDOW OF ADULATION

THE BEGGAR IDOLIZES EVERYONE, THE
RICH MAN HIMSELF

THERE WILL NEVER EXIST MEN AS GODS, NO
MATTER HOW MANY WE ALLOW TO RULE

DO I TRULY RECOGNIZE IDOLATRY FOR
WHAT IT IS ?

TEARS

TO THE GOOD CAUSE I BRING TEARS

I BRING MY TEARS TO THE DOORSTEP
OF MY NEIGHBOR

MY TEARS WILL ASSIGN MYSELF TO
MY BROTHER'S PROTECTION

I DO NOT CRY TO THE IDOLS OF MANKIND

WHERE DO I BRING MY TEARS OF JOY ?

TRUTH

TRUTH EXISTS EVEN AGAINST ALL DISBELIEF

IN OUR QUEST FOR TRUTH,
ONLY HONESTY WILL LEAD THE WAY

TRUTH CAN NEVER CHANGE, IT IS AS IT IS

PERFECTION EXISTS IN TRUTH

THE LIE OF THE WORLD IS THAT EACH
MAN ALONE HOLDS THE TRUTH

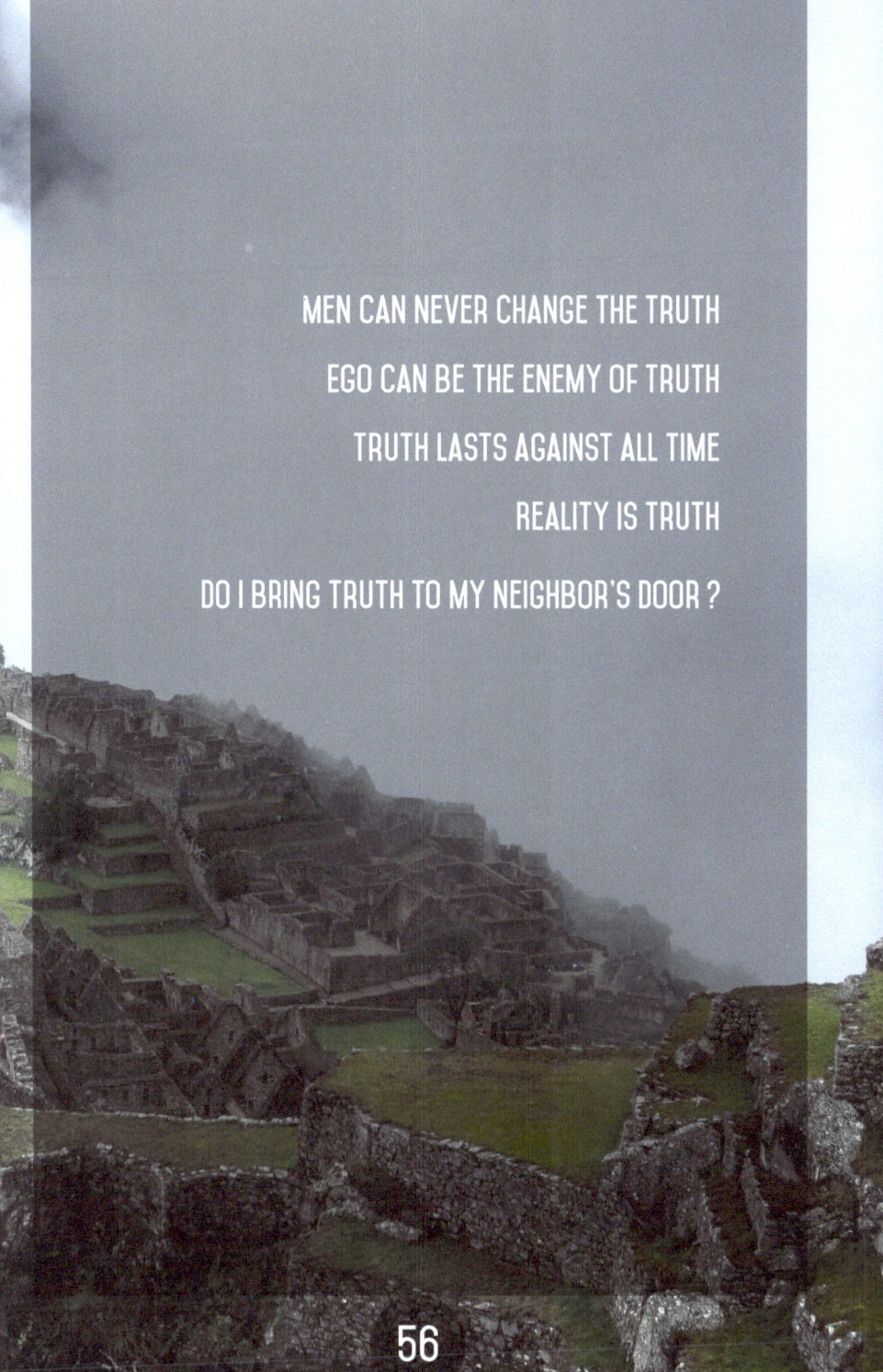

MEN CAN NEVER CHANGE THE TRUTH

EGO CAN BE THE ENEMY OF TRUTH

TRUTH LASTS AGAINST ALL TIME

REALITY IS TRUTH

DO I BRING TRUTH TO MY NEIGHBOR'S DOOR ?

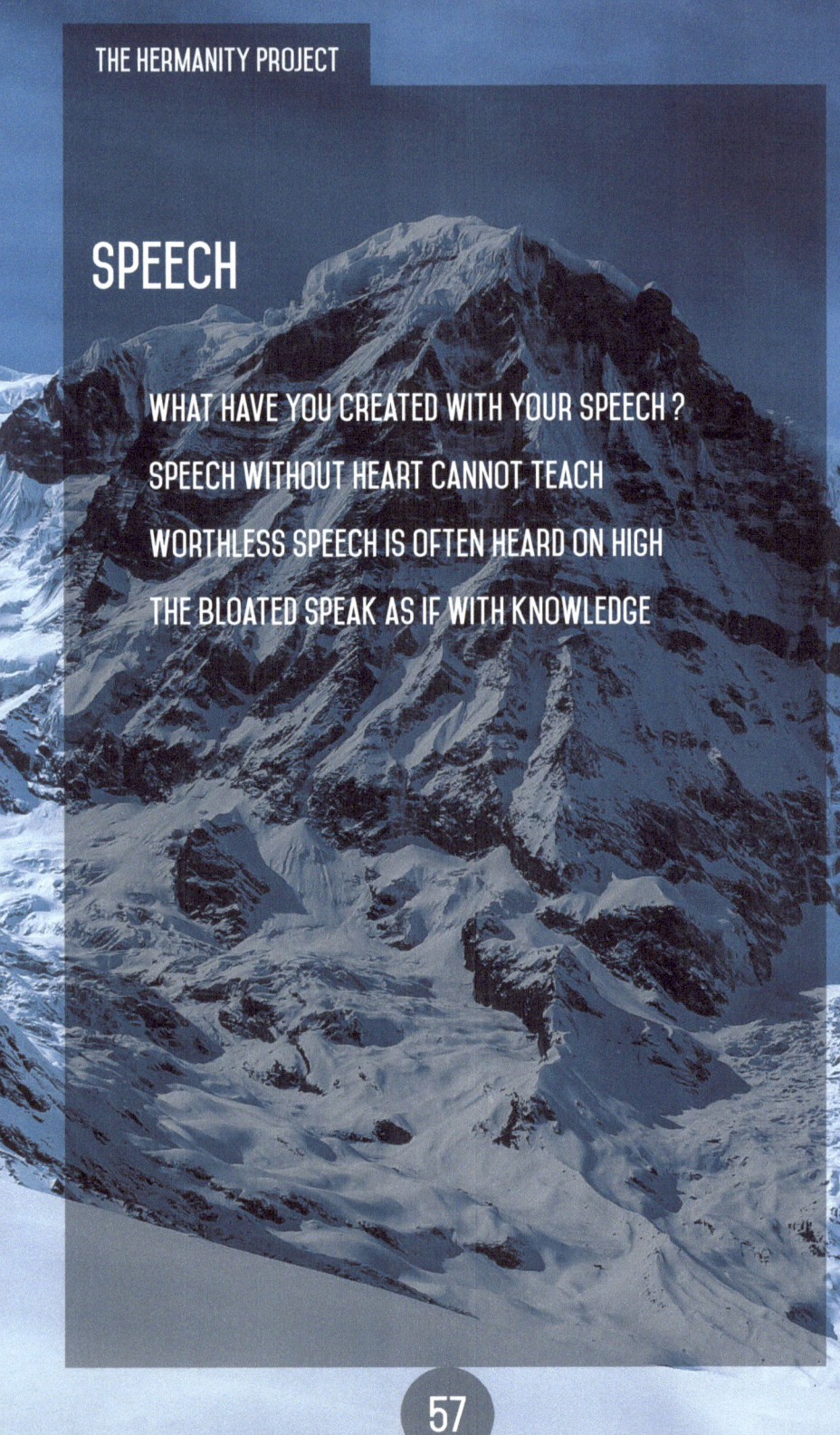

SPEECH

WHAT HAVE YOU CREATED WITH YOUR SPEECH ?

SPEECH WITHOUT HEART CANNOT TEACH

WORTHLESS SPEECH IS OFTEN HEARD ON HIGH

THE BLOATED SPEAK AS IF WITH KNOWLEDGE

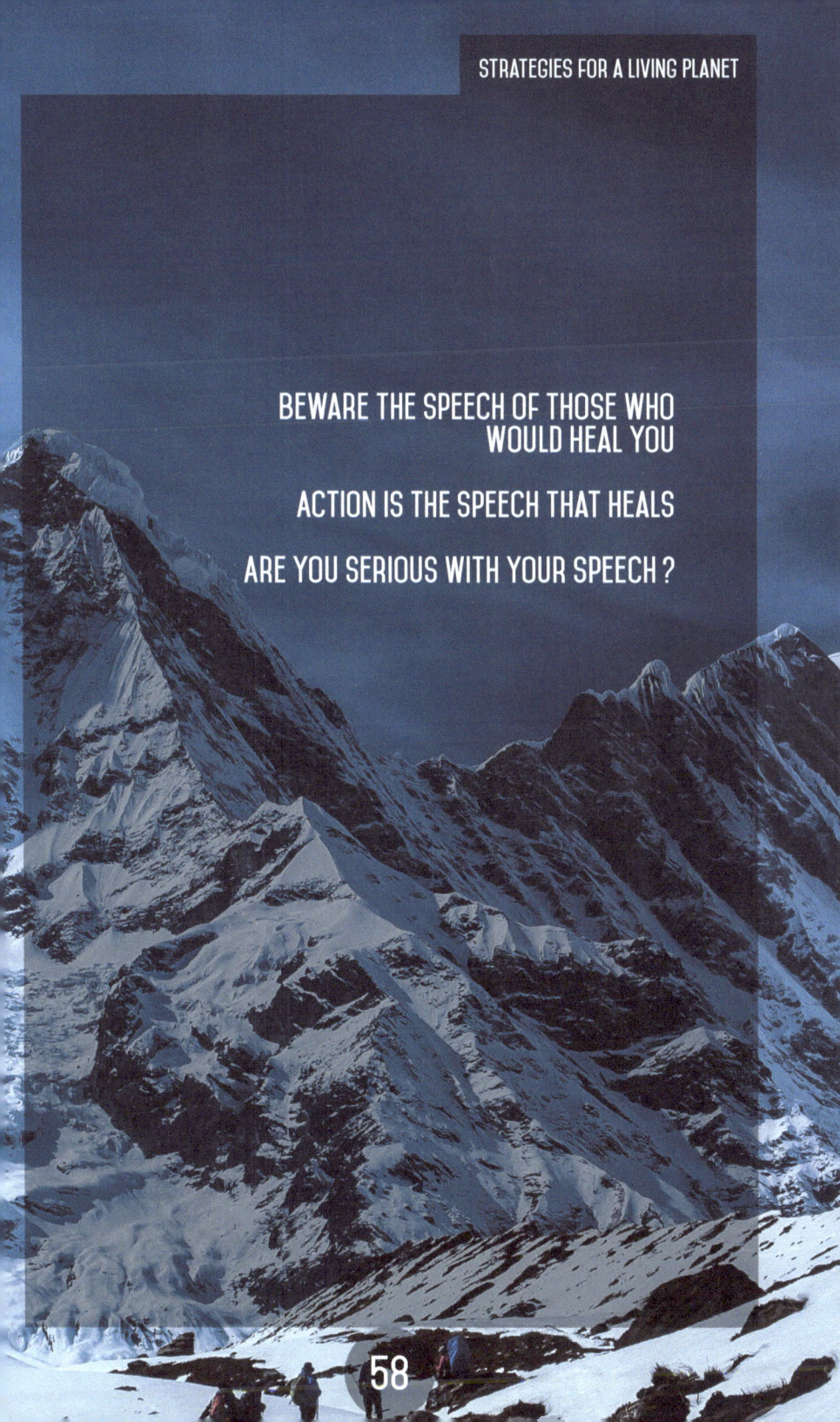

BEWARE THE SPEECH OF THOSE WHO
WOULD HEAL YOU

ACTION IS THE SPEECH THAT HEALS

ARE YOU SERIOUS WITH YOUR SPEECH ?

HONESTY

I COME WITH HONESTY TO MY
NEIGHBOR'S DOOR

HONESTY IS NOT AS I WISH
HONESTY IS TRUTH AS IT IS

DOES YOUR HONESTY SEEK ITS OWN WAY ?

HONESTY WILL SEEK YOUR NEIGHBOR
IN TRUTHFULNESS

EGO CAN BE A CLOUD OF DARKNESS ABOVE
THE LIGHT OF TRUTH

AM I SINCERE IN FINDING MY NEIGHBOR'S PATH ?

PATIENCE

DO I EXIST IN PATIENCE?

AM I PATIENT IN MY NEIGHBOR'S LIFE ?

DO I TRULY BELIEVE I AM WAITING
FOR MY NEIGHBOR ?

WHERE IN MY LIFE DOES MY EGO GO ?

TO LIVE IN THE SIGHT OF MY NEIGHBOR,
I MUST FIRST TAKE HOLD OF MY PATIENCE

WITH STRENGTH I BECOME PATIENCE,
IN EGO I CAN BECOME DARK AS NIGHT

THIS DAY AM I TRULY WILLING
TO PRACTICE PATIENCE ?

AGGRESSION

IF IN OUR TASK WE FAIL TO COMMUNICATE THEN
AGGRESSION CAN NEVER BE TOLERATED

FEROCIOUS AGGRESSION MUST BE MET WITH EQUAL
INTENT FOR FREEDOM IS THE ULTIMATE REWARD

THE WISE SEEK UNDERSTANDING AND RESTRAINT
THE FOOL SEEKS CHAOS AND DESTRUCTION
THE WISE WILL NEVER TOLERATE SUCH FOOLS

THE PEACE THAT WE STRIVE FOR
WILL NOT LEAD US AS LAMBS TO THE SLAUGHTER

HEMANITY'S EXISTENCE AND FREEDOM WILL ALWAYS
COME AT A COST

WHAT THEN ARE WE WILLING TO SPEND IN PURSUIT
OF SUCH FREEDOM ?

FINIS

ABOUT
THE
AUTHOR

Michael Gione - having lived with Tourettes Syndrome and Bipolar disorder for more than 40 years, strives to communicate a message of tolerance, awakening, and unity. Also the author of the book Your Employees... Your Money Making Machine, Gione authors works on business, poetry, and philosophy. Michael lives in Bloomington, Indiana with his wife, two cats, and three dogs.

Mike Gione strives to bring excellence to the world in the form of living strategeies that he hopes will uplift, awaken, and unite humanity.

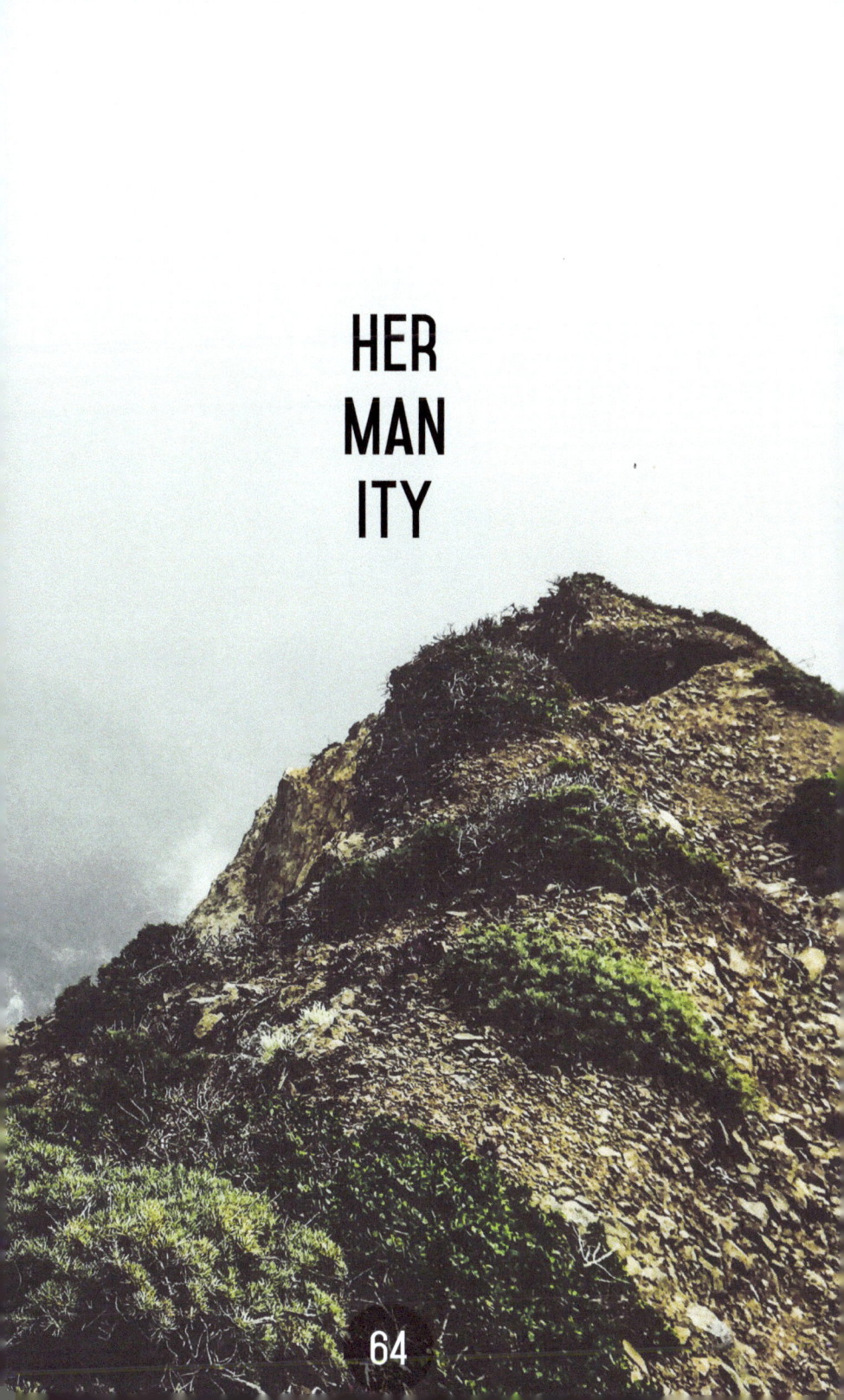

HER
MAN
ITY